To sister Patricia
who could not find the key!

Happy Christmas 94

THE
~ Quiet shore

A Book of Poems and Paintings

by

TOM KERR

Designed by Joanna Martin

PUBLISHED IN 1994 BY PRETANI PRESS

PRETANI PRESS

78 ABBEY STREET BANGOR BT20 4JB

BRITISH CATALOGUING IN PUBLICATION DATA

ISBN 0-948868-21-X

PRINTED IN NORTHERN IRELAND BY

UNIVERSITIES PRESS

for Gail

~

Early Morning Strangford

FOREWORD

That an artist with a gift for expressing himself with eloquence on canvas should also prove to be a poet of gentle perception may surprise some. It may even be the occasion of envy in others. But it should not. For it is the same muse, finding these diverse courses to the sea, which inspires both. Tom Kerr has had the good fortune to live the greater part of his life in a place he so clearly loves. This, therefore, is an affectionate, intensely personal little book.

His nostalgia for what we now regard as simpler, slower times will bring a twinkle to some older eyes, a suspicion of mistiness to others. For it is nature's dispensation, is it not, that we tend to preserve in memory the gilded days, letting go painlessly of those that were less so?

It is a pleasure to wish Tom well with this, his third volume.

ERIC WAUGH

ETERNAL SIGHED THE SEA

Early one morning,
just before the sun was up,
I walked the long straight road
beside the sea.
The lambs, in pairs, black nose to black nose,
sheltered cosy, calling, crying.
Here and there a lark would rise
to start his early song;
and all along the way
the wind made barbed wire fretted lace,
black, blue and white,
of man's discarded plastic waste.

Showing off his speed to me,
a hooded crow
made straight his path into the light.
And ever on my right,
like Sinai's distant voice,
eternal sighed the sea.

THIS MORNING

I saw the robin this morning,

moving through the January branches

of my willow tree.

I saw the fading, full-round moon,

pale as a dying sigh,

Cave Hill, snow-topped, holding at its feet

a thousand tiny homes,

the winter Lough, ice cold, the winter sky.

And on my cheek,

and in my rattling bones,

I felt the cruel blast,

but took some hope to see

along the frosted bough,

the new buds formed,

in nature's promise sure,

that Spring would come at last.

"*...the wicket painted on a gable wall*"

AFTER SCHOOL

I will swim with you again
in the grey-green waters
that lap and lie against our shore.
I will climb with you the tall trees,
and know each branch, each bend, each crook.
I'll find my pockets bulging, stuffed again,
with unripe hazels from the Golf Links glen.
Come January, hunkered down,
I'll slide the icy length of Patton's Hill,
and know again a faint unspoken chill,
scaling Grainger's Quarry flanks,
rock rising steep from mossy banks,
when fingers, arms, and legs and toes
hold tight until I've passed the scary part.

And (serve me right)
the quaking heart,
as furtive, through the hedge's gap,
I think we have been caught at apple stealing.
Again I'll hear the church bells pealing;
somewhere find a tennis ball
for test match cricket,
the wicket painted on a gable wall.

Some day I'll do these things with you again,
before they close the iron door
on boyhood dreams for evermore.

THE THIRTEENTH OF JULY
The Quiet Shore

On that day
we took the train to Craigavad,
my birthday treat,
and made our way, all laden,
to the quiet shore.
We gathered twigs to make a fire
between some chosen stones,
flat-topped to hold the black tea-pot;
and sheltered, smoky, from each summer shower.

Since those far days,
it seems that I alone remain
to walk that shore.
And if I see, cold black and grey,
the embers of a picnic fire,
some distant memory stirs in me,
and I can hear above the waves,
forgotten voices murmuring,
echoes from a bygone day.

SPENCER STREET

The terraced houses straggled
down the street where I was born,
red brick, grey stuccoed family homes,
the chimney sweep's, the sweetie shop,
the milkman's yard.
And on the sunny side,
door steps and window sills,
where we could sit, our homeworks done,
and watch the cows come home
to Granda Thompson's byre.
Or 'hang behind' the binman's cart,
and yell 'Old Rags'
in chorus with the beggar man.

Now that side is graced with maisonettes,
flat-roofed and plastic-wrapped.
No cows, no pigs, no hens,
no horses stamping at the kerbs,
no gas street lamps to swing on.
Here and there,
all strange and out of time,
stands someone from those early days,
seeking links to form a chain,
a memory to cling on.

Redburn Walk

Holywood from Kinnegar

MOLLY

She said she went to school with me,
and as I listened, looked,
a memory stirred,
and I had lost some three score years.
I was back in class again,
learning how to form my "loops",
with head low bent;
and all around the scent
of paper, dust, and chalk.
"I have a list of names," she said,
and there I was, "Tom Kerr",
cheek by jowl with long forgotten friends.
The roll was called,
we shouted "Present!"

"Here Sir, Here!"
not all of us,
for since that time,
a few have passed their last exam,
and slipped this mortal sphere.

A THOUGHT

You and I.

We are part of some eternal union,

a fusion

from beyond the edge of time,

set to walk, and think, and quest,

and ever seeking,

never rest.

Now and then

the veil, the vaporous skein

is gently drawn aside,

but only far enough

to show the faintest edge of glory past,

wherein we all were meant to dwell,

a garden blanketed with love,

which we have since denied.

MY BIRTHDAY

From some abyss,

through all the rutted roads of time,

a breathing form,

I came to this.

Now, close to my allotted span,

I many learned books can scan,

yet not resolve the mystery,

of why I happened to be me.

CULTRA

Here, as boys, we swam,
bravely, bravely, after school.
Even when the days were cold,
we walked, goose-pimpled, noisy, bold,
into the Lough's green waves,
salt in our eyes, our mouths, our ears.
Sometimes then, slight fears
that we might fail to make the shore.
We always did,
to share the one and only towel,
wet and tattered,
flailing arms, teeth that chattered.

And at the end the homeward ride
on cherished bikes.
And, scarce concealed,
a little bit of boyish pride.

Cultra
"Here, as boys, we swam..."

A METEOR SHOWER ~ 1933 and 1993

"Watch out to-night!
You'll see the shooting stars,
a galaxy of streaming light."
So we were told,
for all the men of science knew
our planet earth
some stellar dust was passing through,
the remnants of a comet's tail.
But though we gazed
through skeins of cloud
for hours on end,
we saw no heaven shower.
Our vigil was to no avail.

Yet three-score years ago,
with no prediction that I know,
we children stood in Spencer Street,
our upturned faces rapt and white,
and saw the sky's vast dome
alive with falling stars,
a miracle! a shower of light!

PROGRESS?

I have changed my terraced home
with no mod cons,
for one that sits among the trees,
and boasts a modest patch of grass,
edged all around with shrubs and flowers.
No draughty sashes rattle in the west'ring wind,
for all is plastic now,
and double-glazed to keep inside the heat
from gas-fired boiler, thermostat controlled,
how neat!

And yet I miss
the battered sofa by the fire,
the white scrubbed table with its single drawer,
Trixie's kennel in the yard.
And oh I find it hard
to reconcile this shallow savoir faire,
with humble loyalties that I knew there.

Wag and Susie

Snow Children

TIME'S RECOMPENSES

Sitting at our homework,
while the kitchen clock,
with its uneven tick,
kept its uneven time,
struggling to each wheezing chime;
and out beyond the rattling pane
the back yard wall,
a patch of grey careering sky,
nothing but darkness, wind, and rain.
"Keep at it boys,
you'll build yourselves a more enduring place
than I have had to face."

How could he know
that you and I and everyone
beneath the sun
would hearken back in years long after,
yearning for those early days,
the sound of voices clothed with laughter?

THE DAY OF THE HORSE

Beside the bridge,
close by the steeply curving, cobbled bend,
the great horse, waiting, stood:
and when along the grey quayside
a heavy laden cart appeared,
they hooked him to his mate,
and both together pulled and strained,
with clashing hooves
striking sparks from iron shoes.

And then, one day, he fell,
and lay with frightened, rolling eyes,
and watching we were frightened too.
But carters' men, who knew such things,
gathered round, and loosed his reins,
and spread the granite setts with sacks
to give his striking feet a grip,
and yelled and heaved,
and got him upright once again.

They do not need him now.
Ten thousand cars a day,
race and screech across the bridge,
on asphalt roads, as smooth as silk.
He and his man are long since gone,
to lend a hand in brighter day.

Day of the Storm

Before the Wind

DINOSAURS

They roamed the earth
a hundred million years ago.
They did not know
their likeness would appear
on lollipops and chocolate bars,
on pencils, pens, and Christmas cards.
And they were not aware that some day
puny man would stare
at bits and pieces of their ancient bones,
recovered from the earth;
that he would make, for everyone to see,
great moving pictures, oh so real,
of how they used to be! ·

Some day now,
we'll dig into the hidden earth,
or excavate a few more sandy shelves.
Perhaps we'll find the remnants
of a creature still unknown:
or could it be
that we might even find ourselves.

RUGBY

We played our rugby
on the steeply sloping pitch at Sullivan.
Posts for ever slightly skew,
and well we knew
the muddy patch,
half-way down the left hand side,
stay clear of it!
The German prisoners of war,
standing by the barbed wire fence,
silent watched our schoolboy games.

But I remember long before all that,
seeing the big strong men
playing their last game,
before they went to war.

When they returned,
(not all of them)
they were welcomed to the first fifteen,
and, changing in the old tin hut,
we younger ones were moved aside,
and in the second row
our scarcely stubbled cheeks
were treated to a harsher game.
The smell of Guinness, mud, and sweat,
in memory fills my nostrils yet.

Now togs have been replaced by strip:
the fields are drained and flat,
with upright posts:
and other lads have gone to other wars.

ACROSS THE FIELDS

In the wee pub,
standing at the gate,
or feeding the hens,
they tell us that she is dying.
"In that cottage over there across the fields,
they're waiting, waiting till the spirit yields."

Another day,
too wet to cut the hay below the hill.
"They're waiting, waiting still."

The doctor and the priest have been.
The scene
now holds a quiet, calmer air,

and down the narrow lane
from near and far,
they come,
on foot, by car.
"She's gone - she's gone at last," they say.
And when she passed
a gleam of sunlight burst on Lenan's strand,
and spread a golden light across the land.

Across the Fields

SEEING

Can you see

the path each snowflake treads

when passing through the winter sky;

the pattern of a blackbird's song?

And high beyond the clouds,

where ghosts of love flit in the sunlit air,

I wonder if you have eyes to see

the haloed circle, shining bright,

around an angel's head,

or trembling signs of life renewed

in harvest fields of man's great hope,

when gentle breaths have faltered, fled.

THE PEBBLE

I, like many a one before me,

picked a pebble from the strand,

to marvel at its smooth, round form;

in its colours see the sea,

the gentle contours of the land.

It sudden seemed,

that in my hand,

I held the whole round world,

with all its problems, hopes and fears.

I was frightened then,

and gently placed it with its fellow men,

lest it, like me, became all flawed:

lest it should think,

if it could think,

that I was God.

Girl at the Window

So Faintly Drawn

SO FAINTLY DRAWN

Why did my paintbrush linger on the paper here?

I had no thought to paint a figure in.

Yet all the while I dreamed of you

within the scene,

against the mid-day sky,

in summer's dappled green.

Long afterwards when autumn's chill held sway,

I chanced upon my work,

where it, discarded long ago, still lay,

and saw, so faintly drawn,

your well-known form, with sun-bright eyes.

I pondered much what hand had placed you there,

what mind had framed these mysteries.

JUST ANOTHER DAY

Don't worry.

Don't get so upset my friend.

A broken wineglass or a broken heart.

Neither a beginning nor an end.

Why don't you sit down

in a corner where the sun shines

like next door's cat.

Put on your floppy hat

and close your eyes.

If you hear some sad sighs

pretend they're not your own,

and say

"Why should I make moan.

Perhaps, against the odds,

I'll live to fight another day."

Mountain Shepherd

Walking the Dogs

THE ROAD TO BANGOR

Take the road,

take the road to Bangor,

this January day.

See a thousand broad-winged rooks,

black confetti in the sky,

sweeping brown ploughed fields,

furrows straight as any die;

Helen's gentle profiled tower,

in the midst of leafless trees;

placid winter sheep,

grazing frozen winter leas;

and in letters written large,

on a red barn wall,

"God sent his only son,

for sinners one and all"

KNOWLEDGE

Someone told me that the world was round.

Well fancy that!

I always thought that it was flat.

(Apart from minor bumps and holes,

and flatter portions at the poles.)

I wonder now, did Jesus know,

when walking, talking here below.

He surely must,

for after all, He was the son of God,

who made us from primeval dust.

He never mentioned it I see,

when leaving truths for you and me.

Perhaps he thought it more important

that we should walk that extra mile,

and greet our neighbour with a smile;

That knowledge stems from heaven above,

but scores few points compared with love.

THE FIVE TO NINE

In my dreams

it seems

I must go back to work again;

catch the train

at five to nine;

hear it thunder down the line,

run the length of Spencer Street,

final dash across the Square,

past the soldier cast in bronze,

futile bayonet in the air:

just in time to hear and see

my old friend No.23,

belching smoke, and hissing steam,

pull away to Belfast town,

and leave me once again, cast down,

awaking from my dream.

The Five to Nine

THE SKY

This is my sky,
at dead of night,
when the moon is dark,
and the Milky Way
is a path of light
to a million stars.

This is my sky,
when the dawn creeps cold
behind the hills,
when the trees are stark,
and bed seems warm
to limbs grown old.

This is my sky,
when the sun sings high,
and the grass is green;
when the sand is white,
and the sea is blue.
This is my sky,
I will share it with you.

Paint the sky grey,

for that's how it is today.

Let the grey run into the sea and the land,

for that's how it is today.

Paint the bleak trees,

fretted and torn in the rip of the wind;

boys and girls,

homeward making their rain-drenched way

from school.

"You're soaked to the skin"

their mothers will say;

spats of sleet on the window pane;

flicking lights on the aeroplane

going in to land.

Paint these things now,

just as they are,

for that is how it is today.

Cattle by a Stream

Winter on the Moors

MUM

I did not know that she was dying,

until one day she told me so,

when passing by her bed.

"Don't be daft" I said,

for well I knew that mothers could not die.

But I was cheated,

this one did,

and left me as a lad

to place a shilling bunch of daffodils

upon her early grave,

each Saturday,

before the rugby game.

SEPTEMBER STORM

Never such rain,

such rain in Donegal.

And though we walked in Autumn gold,

the signs of last week's storm were everywhere,

with landslips on the mountain's flank,

low flooded fields,

and, saddest sight of all,

standing dead and dank,

in Michael's field,

the scythe-cut stooks of corn,

stark in their midst a warning sign,

no longer heeded, needed now,

a magpie by the farmer slain,

and hanging from a gallows bough.

Eternal sighed the Sea

Snow in the Suburbs

AT THE EDGE OF THE WATER

I have walked where the shadows of love

from another day

lay on this sand.

I have heard in the plangent roar

of this great sea,

the sounding bells of eternity.

I have looked beyond these skies,

to a land where myriad suns shall rise.

I have touched an angel's hand.

I will hold it close,

when I leave this land.

NIGHT TIME TAKE OFF

The giant plane,
freed from each fuel-feeding cord,
curved across the wet tarmac,
and, like some gorged leviathan,
obedient to a tiny child,
followed, through the windswept dark,
two tiny hand-held glow worm lights,
until it reached the very spot
where it could shrug aside such aids;
then, having braced each sinew taut,
it roared and roared,
and louder roared,
and so displayed its awful power,
then hurtled madly into night,
and cracked the sky with dreadful noise.

Cocooned within its belly warm,
we hundreds sat,
and thought our thoughts.
And far below, in Lego homes,
the people heard the jumbo jet,
and thought their thoughts,
and watched T.V.

HALF WAY TO THE TOP OF THE HILL

I sometimes sit on the seat
half-way to the top of the hill
to gather my breath.
And I can see
beyond the giant cranes
the city sleep, or seem to sleep,
with no apparent thought
for any violent death
that I might read about next day.
And I can touch
the messages of love
so crudely cut into the plank on which I rest.

And I can be,
if so I wish,
and so the sky, and trees, and simple hope
will let me be,
just for an instant,
blest.

Half Way to the top of the Hill

A GARLAND OF FLOWERS

"Take these poems," he said,

"and make of them a garland."

"Poems are only words," she said.

Take these poems,

a garland of flowers for the spring.

Let them sing to you

of sun-bright hours,

of azure skies and heaven's bowers.

Let them rise like love

through the pulse-swift air,

like the beating wings

of a thousand birds.

"Poems are only words" she said.

Take these poems,

a garland of flowers for the spring.

Let them sing to you of sad-sweet days,

when the shattered air

seems mocked by praise,

and the hoped for prize

is carried away

on the beating wings

of a thousand birds.

"Poems are only words," she said,

"Poems are only words."

ONE EVENING

I sat and watched
until the bare-branched trees
had faded into darkening night.
The street lamps brighter glowed,
and echoed tiny sparks of light
a dozen miles away.
I saw the smooth descending grace
of yet another homeward flight,
and heard my evening paper
rattle in the letter box.

And when I looked again,
the scene outside my window pane had gone.
I saw myself, pen poised,
reflected in the glass;
yet not myself, but someone, somehow strange,
not known to me.
What matter!
Night had come,
and I had watched again
the daylight pass.

Waiting

Dusk

AN AUTUMN EVENING

The way was steep, all weary I
was glad to rest against the gate.
Cool evening light held still the sky.
A tractor in the distance, late,
was gathering the harvest home,
when from the air, all golden, free,
I heard a voice soft speak to me.

The metal, harsh and rude beneath my hand,
was cold as ice.
The full round moon crept high above the sheaves.
The fading world-born sounds were all forgot.
I heard your voice soft speak to me!

BLACKBIRD AT DUSK

Is that the blackbird's song I hear,

from the top of the orchard wall?

Isn't this the place where we heard him sing

when dusk was beginning to fall?

There is only the sound of the wind in the trees

and around the chimneys tall.

Is that the blackbird I see again

against the sunset sky?

Isn't this the place where we often stood

together, in days gone by?

It is only a trick of the light, I said.

The blackbird has gone, as must you and I.

Let us walk this path a little way,

he might sing for us another day.

THE DAISY CHAIN

Sitting in the meadow,

under a warm blue sky,

I said,

"Gather me daisies,

and I'll show you

how to make a daisy chain."

"Split the stem with your nail, like so,

thread the next one through, and go

right on to the very end,

and then I'll tell you what to do:

first and last together tend

and gently push the flower head through."

As I placed the chain

round the sun-browned brow,

I thought,

just as I am telling you now,

so I was told

long years ago,

and so will you

your children show.

Gather me Daisies

INIS EOGHAIN

They look at me,

the young men of Ireland,

and I see in their shadowed eyes,

the rock strewn farm,

the dye-blotched sheep,

black tarred roofs

that shelter, far into the night,

their restless dancing feet.

They look at me,

the old men of Ireland,

and I see in their shadowed eyes,

the moss-wet stones of their ruined walls,

the white turf ashes,

gold bands on the wrists of their sons returned,

the tearing sea,

over the rocks the sea birds wheeling,

sea birds crying,

myself, like them,

for I am kin to them,

for ever sighing.

NOTHING IS KNOWN

If I seem to lean towards the final day,

it is because I grow weary,

and although the battle is still fought,

it is fought with less vigour now.

Nothing is certain any more.

Nothing is known.

The pebble washed along the shore

holds in its heart,

all turned to stone,

a creature from the dawn of time,

tossed by the self-same wave,

and out beyond the dark horizon line

the searched for love still dwells,

just as it did of yore.

A Lonely Place